NLP For Beginners

[RS Johnson]

Copyright © 2012 **RS Johnson**

All rights reserved.

Table of Contents

Introduction 6

History of NLP 7

    The first phase (Machine Translation Phase) lasted from the late 1940s to the late 1960s. 7

    Second Phase (AI-Inspired Phase) – Late 1960s to late 1970s 8

    Third Phase (Grammatico-logical Phase) – Late 1970s to late 1980s 8

    Fourth Phase (Lexical & Corpus Phase) – The 1990s 9

Study of Human Languages 10

    Ambiguity and Uncertainty in Language 10

    Lexical Ambiguity 10

    Syntactic Ambiguity 10

    Semantic Ambiguity 11

    Anaphoric Ambiguity 11

    Pragmatic ambiguity 11

NLP Phases 12

    Morphological Processing 12

    Syntax Analysis 12

    Semantic Analysis 12

    Pragmatic Analysis 12

What are Tokens, Corpus, and Engrams? 13

What is Tokenization? 13

What is Whitespace Tokenization? 13

What is Normalization? 14

What is Stemming? 15

What is Lemmatization? 15

Tags for Parts of Speech (PoS) in Natural Language Processing 17

What is Constituency Grammar? 18

What is Dependency Grammar? 19

What is the history of Natural Language Processing? 20

How does Natural Language Processing work? . 21

Why is it necessary to advance in the field of NLP? 23

What can natural language processing do? 24

What are some examples of NLP applications? . 24

How to learn Natural Language Processing (NLP)? 24

Available Open-Source software in NLP Domain ... 26

What are Regular Expressions? 26

What is Text Wrangling? 26

What factors influence the quantity and quality of cleaning? ... 27

How do we define text cleansing? ... 27

Sentence splitter ... 28

What are the various types of stemmers? ... 28

What is Stop Word Removal? ... 29

What is Rare Word Removal? ... 29

What is Spell Correction? ... 30

What is Dependency Parsing? ... 30

Machine Translation ... 32

Types of Machine Translation Systems ... 32

Direct MT Approach ... 32

Interlingua Approach ... 32

Transfer Approach ... 33

Empirical MT Approach ... 33

Automatic Summarization ... 34

Conclusion ... 35

Introduction

According to industry estimates, just 21% of accessible data is in an organized format. Data is created while we speak, tweet, post messages on WhatsApp, and engage in other activities. The majority of this data comes in the form of text, which is very unstructured. Even though it contains high-dimensional data, the information contained within it is not readily accessible until it is manually processed (read and comprehended) or analyzed by an automated system. It is critical to understand Natural Language Processing fundamentals to get meaningful and actionable insights from text data (NLP). Language is a kind of communication that allows us to talk, read, and write. For example, we think, make judgments, plan, and do other things in natural language, specifically, in words. However, the key question in this AI era is if people can communicate comparably with machines.

To put it another way, can humans interact with computers in their native language? It is difficult to build NLP applications because computers require organized input, but human speech is unstructured and frequently confusing. In this respect, Natural Language Processing (NLP) is the subfield of Computer Science, particularly Artificial Intelligence (AI), concerned with allowing computers to comprehend and process human language. NLP's major technical goal would be to program computers to analyze and interpret massive amounts of natural language data.

In this book, we will properly go through the fundamentals of several Natural Language Processing methods.

History of NLP

We have separated NLP's history into four stages. The stages each have their issues and styles.

The first phase (Machine Translation Phase) lasted from the late 1940s to the late 1960s.

This phase's work was mostly focused on machine translation (MT). This was a moment of excitement and hope.

Let us now examine everything that the first phase contained-

- Following Booth and Richens' inquiry and Weaver's memorandum on machine translation in 1949, NLP research began in the early 1950s.
- The Georgetown-IBM project presented a modest attempt at automated translation from Russian to English in 1954.
- The journal MT (Machine Translation) began publication the same year.
- The primary international conference on machine translation (MT) took place in 1952, followed by the second in 1956.
- The work presented at the Teddington International Conference on Machine Translation of Languages and Applied Language Analysis in 1961 was the pinnacle of this period.

Second Phase (AI-Inspired Phase) – Late 1960s to late 1970s

Most of the effort focused on world knowledge and its function in building and manipulating meaning representations during this phase. As a result, this phase is also known as the AI-flavored phase.

The period included the following -
- The work on the issues of addressing and creating data or knowledge bases began in early 1961. AI had an impact on this work.
- A BASEBALL question-answering system was also developed the same year. This system's input was limited, and the language processing involved was straightforward.
- Minsky described a far more sophisticated system (1968). Compared to the BASEBALL question-answering system, this system identified and accommodated the need for knowledge base inference in understanding and reacting to language input.

Third Phase (Grammatico-logical Phase) – Late 1970s to late 1980s

This phase is known as the grammatical-logical phase. Due to the previous phase's failure of the practical system construction phase, the researchers shifted their focus to applying logic for knowledge representation and reasoning in AI.

The third phase included the following:
- By the end of the decade, the grammatical-logical method had provided us with strong general-purpose sentence processors such as SRI's Core Language

Engine and Conversation Representation Theory, which allowed us to tackle more prolonged discourse.
- We obtained some practical resources and tools during this phase, such as parsers, such as Alvey Natural Language Tools, and more operational and commercial systems, such as those used for database queries.
- Lexicon's work in the 1980s also led in the direction of a grammatical-logical approach.

Fourth Phase (Lexical & Corpus Phase) – The 1990s

This is referred to as a lexical and corpus phase. The phase had a lexicalized approach to grammar that emerged in the late 1980s and gained growing prominence. With the development of machine learning techniques for language processing in this decade, a revolution occurred in natural language processing.

Study of Human Languages

Language is both an essential component of our life and the most fundamental feature of our conduct. We may encounter it primarily in two ways: written and spoken. It is a method of passing down information from one generation to the next in written form. It is the principal channel via which humans organize their day-to-day activities in spoken form. Language is researched in a variety of academic fields. So every sector will have its own set of problems and solutions to those problems.

Ambiguity and Uncertainty in Language

As commonly employed in natural language processing, ambiguity is defined as being understood in more than one manner. In layman's words, ambiguity is the ability to be understood in more than one way. Natural language is rife with ambiguity. The following sorts of ambiguity exist in NLP:

Lexical Ambiguity

Lexical ambiguity refers to the ambiguity of a single word. For instance, you might use the word silver as a noun, an adjective, or a verb.

Syntactic Ambiguity

When a statement is processed in multiple ways, this type of ambiguity develops. For example, "The man noticed the girl with the telescope." It's unclear if the man observed the child while carrying a telescope or via his telescope.

Semantic Ambiguity

When the meaning of the words themselves might be misunderstood, this type of ambiguity emerges. Semantic ambiguity occurs when a statement contains an unclear term or phrase. For example, the statement "The vehicle struck the pole while it was moving" has semantic ambiguity since it may be interpreted as "The car hit the pole while it was moving" or "The automobile hit the pole while the pole was moving."

Anaphoric Ambiguity

The employment of anaphora entities in a conversation causes this type of ambiguity. For instance, the horse galloped up the hill. It was quite steep. It quickly grew weary. In two cases, the anaphoric reference of "it" creates ambiguity.

Pragmatic ambiguity

This type of ambiguity refers to a scenario in which the context of a statement allows for numerous interpretations. In layman's terms, pragmatic ambiguity occurs when a statement is not explicit. For example, the phrase "I like you too" might be interpreted in several ways: I like you (just like you like me), I like you (just like you like me), I like you (exactly like you like me), I like you (just like you like me), I like you (just as you like (just like someone else does).

NLP Phases

The figure below depicts the stages or logical steps in natural language processing-

Morphological Processing

It is the initial stage of NLP. This phase aims to separate chunks of linguistic input into tokens that correspond to paragraphs, phrases, and words. For example, "uneasy" may be split into two sub-word tokens as "un-easy."

Syntax Analysis

It is the NLP's second phase. This phase's goal is twofold: to determine whether or not a phrase is well constructed and divide it into a structure that demonstrates the syntactic links between the various components. So, for example, a syntax analyzer or parser might reject the statement "The boy goes to school."

Semantic Analysis

It is the third stage of the NLP process. The goal of this step is to extract precise meaning, or dictionary meaning, from the text. Then, the text is reviewed for meaning. A semantic analyzer, for example, might reject a phrase like "hot ice cream."

Pragmatic Analysis

It is NLP's fourth phase. The pragmatic analysis matches the real objects/events in a particular context with the object references collected in the previous step (semantic analysis). For example, the statement "Place the banana in the basket on the shelf" might have two semantic interpretations, and the pragmatic analyzer will pick one of them.

What are Tokens, Corpus, and Engrams?

A corpus is a list of written documents, such as news or tweets containing Twitter data. So the corpus is made up of documents, which are made up of paragraphs, which are made up of phrases, and sentences are made up of even smaller units called Tokens.
Tokens might be words, sentences, or Engrams, which are defined as groups of n words.
Consider the following statement as an example:
"I love my phone. "
In this sentence, the uni-grams are (n=1): I, love, my, phone
Di-grams are (n=2): love my, I love, my phone
And tri-grams(n=3) are:- I love my, love my phone
So, uni-grams represent one word, di-grams represent two words together, and tri-grams represent three words.

What is Tokenization?

Let's talk about Tokenization right now. Tokenization is the method of properly breaking down a text item into smaller pieces known as tokens. Words, numerals, engrams, and symbols are all examples of tokens. Whitespace Tokenization is the most widely used tokenization technique.

What is Whitespace Tokenization?

Unigram tokenization is another term for it. During this procedure, the entire text is divided into words by removing white spaces.

In a sentence, for example, "I traveled to New York to play football."

This will be divided into the following tokens: "I," "went," "to," "New York," "to," "play," and "football."

Because the tokenization procedure was based solely on whitespaces, "New York" is not further divided.

Regular Expression Tokenization is another tokenization procedure that uses a regular expression pattern to obtain the tokens. For example, consider the following string, which has various delimiters such as a comma, a semi-colon, and white space.

Sentence= ""Football, Cricket; Golf Tennis"

pre-split (r' [; \s]', Sentence

Tokens= ""Football""," Cricket", "Golf", "Tennis"

We may separate the text using Regular Expressions by supplying a dividing pattern.

Tokenization can take place at the phrase, global, or even character level.

What is Normalization?

Normalization is the next method. A Morpheme is the basic form of a word in the realm of linguistics and NLP. Morphemes, which are the basic form of the word, and Inflectional forms, simply suffixes, and prefixes appended to morphemes, are the two main components of a token. For example, consider the term Antinationalist, composed of the inflectional forms Anti, and it's and the morpheme national. The process of transforming a token to its basic form is known as normalization. The inflection from a word is eliminated during the normalization process to retrieve the base form. As a result, the nation is the normalized version of anti-nationalism. Normalization is beneficial for lowering the number of unique tokens in the text, eliminating word variants, and deleting unnecessary information. Stemming and Lemmatization are two popular approaches for normalizing.

What is Stemming?

Stemming is a simple rule-based procedure for eliminating inflectional forms from a token, and the outputs are the world's stem.

Because their inflection form is eliminated, words like "laughing," "laughed," "laughs," and "laugh" will all become "laugh," which is their stem.

Stemming is not a good normalization technique since it might create terms that are not in the dictionary. For example, consider the following sentence: "His teams are not winning."

The tokens we will receive after stemming are "hello", "team", "are", "not", and "winn".

The term "wine" is not a normal word, and "hello" altered the meaning of the entire phrase.

What is Lemmatization?

Lemmatization, on the other hand, is a step-by-step procedure for eliminating a word's inflection forms. It employs vocabulary, word structure, part of speech tags, and grammatical relationships. The result of Lemmatization is a root word known as a lemma. For instance, Am, Are, and Is >> Be Running, Ran, Run >> Run

Furthermore, because Lemmatization is a systematic procedure, one may provide the part of the speech tag for the desired term. Lemmatization will only be done if the given word contains the correct part of the speech tag. So, for example, if we try to lemmatize the term running as a verb, we get to run. However, if we attempt to lemmatize the same word running as a noun, it will not be transformed. A detailed description of how Lemmatization works to eliminate inflection forms from a word-

Let's have a look at some of the syntax and structural characteristics of text objects now. Then, grammar and part of speech tags will be discussed.

Tags for Parts of Speech (PoS) in Natural Language Processing

Part of speech tags, also known as PoS tags, are the qualities of words that identify their major context, purpose, and usage in a phrase. The following are some examples of widely used parts of speech tags: Nouns are words that define an item or thing; verbs are words that specify an action; and adjectives or adverbs are words that function as modifiers, quantifiers, or intensifiers in a phrase. Every word in a phrase will be paired with an appropriate part of the speech tag, for as "David purchased a new laptop from the Apple shop."

Every word in the following phrase is connected with a part of the speech tag that describes its purpose.

In this example, "David" contains an NNP tag, showing that it is a proper noun, "has" and "purchased" are verbs, indicating that they are actions, and "laptop" and "Apple store" are nouns, with "new" serving as an adjective to change the context of laptop.

The relationships of words with the other words in the phrase define part of speech tags. To determine a word's part of speech tags, machine learning models or rule-based models are used. Penn provides the most widely used part of speech tagging notations. For example, tagging a portion of a sentence.

Part of speech tags have a wide range of applications and are utilized in various activities, including text cleaning, feature engineering, and word sense disambiguation. Consider the following two sentences:

Sentence 1: "Please **book** my flight for New York."
Sentence 2: "I like to properly read a **book** on New York."

The term "book" appears in both phrases, but it is employed as a verb in sentence one, whereas it is used as a noun in sentence two.

Grammar in NLP and its variants- Let's talk about grammar now. Grammar is the set of principles for creating well-structured sentences. Constituency grammar is the initial sort of grammar.

What is Constituency Grammar?

Constituents can be any word, collection of words, or phrase, and the objective of constituency grammar is to arrange every sentence into its constituents using their characteristics. These characteristics are often influenced by their part of speech tags, such as noun or verb phrase identification.

Constituency grammar, for example, states that each phrase may be divided into three constituents: a subject, a context, and an object.

These components can have various values, resulting in different phrases. We have, for example, the following constituents-

Some sentences that may be formed utilizing these elements are as follows:

"The dogs are barking in the park."
"They are eating happily."
"The cats are running since morning."

Another way to properly look at constituency grammar is to define it in terms of part-of-speech tags. For example, say you have a grammatical structure with a [determiner, noun] [adjective, verb] [preposition, determiner, noun] that corresponds to the same sentence: "The dogs are barking in the park."

What is Dependency Grammar?

Dependency Grammar is a form of grammar that asserts that words in a sentence rely on other words in the phrase. For example, in the above line, "barking dog" was mentioned, and the dog was changed by barking since the two had a dependence adjective modifier. Dependency grammar arranges the words in a phrase based on their dependencies. One of the words in a phrase serves as a root, and all of the other words are directly or indirectly related to the root through their dependencies. Dependencies indicate relationships between words in a phrase, and dependency grammars infer the structure and meaning dependencies between the words.

Consider the following sentence: "Analytics Vidhya is the largest community of data scientists and the finest resource for understanding data and analytics."

This sentence's dependency tree looks like this: The root word in this tree is "community," with NN also as part of the speech tag, and every other word in this tree is linked to the root, either directly or indirectly, via a dependency relation such as a direct object, direct subject, modifiers, and so on. These relationships describe each word's responsibilities and functions in the phrase and how several words are linked together. Every dependence may be described as a triplet consisting of a governor, a relation, and a dependent, which implies that the dependent is linked to the governor by relation. In other words, they are the subject, verb, and object, in that order. For example, "Analytics Vidhya is the greatest community of data scientists," according to the same statement.

The subject is "Analytics Vidhya," which is acting as a governor, the verb is "is," which is acting as a relation, and the dependent or object is "the biggest community of data scientists."

Dependency grammars can be applied in a variety of contexts.

- **Named Entity Recognition**– They are used to tackle difficulties involving named entity recognition.
- **Question Answering System**– They may be used to comprehend the relational and structural features of question-answering systems.
- **Coreference Resolution**– They are also employed in coreference resolves, where the objective is to map pronouns to their corresponding noun phrases.
- **Text summarization and Text classification** may also be utilized to solve text summarization difficulties and as features in text classification challenges.

The importance of NLP in today's society is growing. However, with the volume of unstructured data created, it is only efficient to master this ability or at the very least comprehend it to the point that you, as a data scientist, can make some sense of it.

What is the history of Natural Language Processing?

Linguists are those who work on language characterization and the comprehension of language patterns. Computational linguistics took off when the volume of textual data began to skyrocket. Wikipedia is the most comprehensive-textual resource available. Computational linguistics arose from an early interest in comprehending data patterns, Parts-of-Speech (POS) labeling, and simpler data processing for different applications in the banking and financial industries, educational institutions, etc.

How does Natural Language Processing work?

NLP seeks to turn unstructured data into computer-readable language by utilizing natural language characteristics. Machines use complex algorithms to break down any written material to extract useful information from it. The acquired data is then utilized to teach robots natural language reasoning. Natural language processing guides machines by detecting and recognizing data patterns using syntactic and semantic analysis. It consists of the following steps:

Syntax: Natural language processing employs various algorithms to adhere to grammatical norms, which are then utilized to infer meaning from any type of text material. Common syntactic methods include Lemmatization, word segmentation, part-of-speech tagging, parsing, sentence breaking, morphological segmentation, and stemming.

Semantics: This is a rather complex process in which robots attempt to comprehend the meaning of each piece of any information, both individually and in context. Even though semantical analysis has gone a long way since its initial binary disposition, there is still much opportunity for development. One of the key phrases that separate text material into predetermined groupings is NER or Named Entity Recognition. The next phase in the process is word sense disambiguation, which deals with contextual meaning. Natural language creation is the final step in the process, which includes deriving meaning from historical information and converting it into human languages.

Why is natural language processing important?

The quantity of data we create grows by the day, necessitating the analysis and documentation of this data. NLP properly enables computers to read this data and transmit it in human-readable languages.

A large portion of this data is properly unstructured, ranging from medical records to recurring government data. NLP assists computers in inputting data into appropriate forms. Following that, computers analyze documents and speech to extract meaning. Not only is the procedure automated, but it is also near-perfect all of the time.

Why is it necessary to advance in the field of NLP?

NLP is the process of improving computers' ability to interpret human language. Databases are highly organized data types. The Internet, on the other hand, is entirely unstructured with only a few structural components. In this situation, the ultimate objective of NLP is to comprehend and model human language. For example, Google Duplex and Alibaba's voice assistants are on the path to mastering non-linear interactions. Non-linear dialogues are similar to the way humans communicate. In the first phase, we discuss cats, go to Tom, and return to the original issue. The person who is listening realizes the leap that occurs. Computers do not presently have this capacity.

What can natural language processing do?

NLP specialists are now in high demand since the amount of unstructured data available is rapidly rising. This unstructured data properly contains a wealth of information that can help businesses develop and thrive. Monitoring tweet trends, for example, can be used to analyze societal issues and in times of disaster. Thus, knowing and applying NLP is unquestionably a certain way to get into the field of machine learning. Creating an NLP portfolio would greatly enhance the possibilities of a novice breaking into the area of NLP.

What are some examples of NLP applications?

1. Grammarly, Microsoft Word, Google Docs
2. Search engines like DuckDuckGo, Google
3. Voice assistants – Alexa, Siri
4. Newsfeeds- Facebook, Google News
5. Translation systems – Google translate

How to learn Natural Language Processing (NLP)?

First, you must be well-versed in programming languages like Python, Keras, NumPy, and others. You should also understand the fundamentals of text data cleansing, manual Tokenization, and NLTK tokenization. The next part of the process is to pick up the bag-of-words model (with Scikit learn, Keras) and more. Next, learn how the word embedding distribution works and how to create it from scratch in Python. Embedding is a crucial element of NLP because embedding layers assist you in appropriately encoding your text. After you've mastered embedding, go on to text classification, followed by dataset evaluation. And you're ready to go!

Great Learning provides a Deep Learning certificate program that covers all major areas of NLP, such as Recurrent Neural Networks, Common NLP techniques – Bag of words, POS tagging, Tokenization, Sentiment analysis, stop words, Machine translation, Long-short term memory (LSTM), and Word embedding – word2vec, GloVe.

Available Open-Source software in NLP Domain

We will learn about conventional NLP, a subject dominated by clever algorithms designed to tackle various issues. With the advancement of deep neural networks, NLP has followed the same approach to addressing the majority of today's challenges. To ensure that the foundations are grasped, we shall examine conventional algorithms in this post.

We'll go through fundamental topics, including regular expressions, text preparation, POS-tagging, and parsing.

What are Regular Expressions?

Regular expressions are useful for finding patterns in strings. Patterns are often utilized to extract useful information from massive quantities of unstructured data. There are several regular expressions at work.

What is Text Wrangling?

It will be defined as the pre-processing before producing machine-readable and prepared text from raw data.

Text wrangling includes the following processes:

1) text cleansing
2) stop word removal
3) tokenization
4) specific pre-processing
5) stemming or Lemmatization

Text Cleansing

Because of the unstructured nature of the language, text collected from multiple sources contains a lot of noise. Therefore, we must make sense of the raw data's unstructured characteristics after parsing the text from the various data sources. As a result, text cleansing is employed in the majority of cleaning tasks.

What factors influence the quantity and quality of cleaning?
1. Parsing performance
2. External noise
3. Source of data source

Consider a second scenario in which we parse a PDF. There may be loud characters, non-ASCII characters, and so forth. We should delete them before moving on to the next set of activities to have a clean text to work with. When dealing with XML files, we are interested in certain tree components. For example, we modify splitters and are interested in certain columns in the case of databases. In the following part, we will look at splitters.

How do we define text cleansing?
Finally, text cleaning refers to cleaning the text and eliminating the content's noise. Data munging and data wrangling are other terms for the same thing. In a comparable situation, they are used interchangeably.

Sentence splitter

To obtain relevant data from NLP systems, huge amounts of raw text must be divided into sentences. A phrase, on the surface, appears to be the smallest unit of speech. What is the best way to define something like a sentence for a computer? First and foremost, how do we need to find this smallest unit? We require it since it streamlines the procedure. For example, the period can be used as a sentence separator, representing one phrase. To extract dialogues from a paragraph, we look for phrases that include inverted commas or double-inverted commas. A sentence splitter can be as basic as dividing the string on (.) or as complicated as a predictive classifier to detect sentence boundaries.

What are the various types of stemmers?

Porter stemmer employs a greater number of rules and delivers cutting-edge accuracies for languages with fewer morphological variants. If necessary, special stemmers for complicated languages must be created. A basic rule-based stemmer, such as eliminating –s/es, –ing, or –ed, on the other hand, can provide an accuracy of more than 70%.

Snowball stemmers are used for various languages, including Dutch, English, French, German, Italian, Portuguese, Romanian, and Russian.

Current NLP applications often avoid pre-processing steps since they depend on the domain and application of interest. We should avoid stemming when using NLP taggers such as Part of Speech tagger (POS), dependency parser, or NER since it changes the token and might result in an unexpected result.

What is Stop Word Removal?

Stop words are the most frequent word type, yet they rarely add weight or meaning to sentences. Instead, they serve as bridges, ensuring that sentences are grammatically accurate. It is one of the most often utilized pre-processing stages in a variety of NLP applications. Thus, stop-word removal is defined as eliminating terms that often appear in the corpus. The vast majority of articles and pronouns are considered stop words. Stop words have little effect on many activities, such as information retrieval and categorization. As a result, stop-word removal is not necessary for this situation.

On the contrary, stop word removal has a significant influence in several NLP applications. A language's stop word list is a hand-curated list of words that appear often. Most languages have to stop word lists available online. There are several methods for automatically generating the stop word list. Using the term's document frequency is a quick approach to get the stop word list. The existence of words across the corpus is utilized as a signal for the categorization of stopwords. According to research, we acquire the best collection of stop words for a particular corpus. NLTK has a comprehensive list of 22 languages. Consider responding to the following questions.

- What role does stop-word removal play?
- What are some stop-word removal alternatives?

What is Rare Word Removal?

Some extremely distinctive words, such as names, brands, product names, and some noise characters, must be eliminated for various NLP jobs. In the case of text categorization, the usage of names is not a viable choice. Even though we are all aware that Adolf Hitler is connected with carnage, his name is an exception. Names, in general, do not convey emotion; therefore, nouns are considered uncommon words and substituted by a single token. The uncommon words are application-specific and must be picked specifically for each application.

What is Spell Correction?

Finally, spellings in the provided corpus should be verified. The model should not be trained using incorrect spellings since the outputs will be incorrect. Thus, spelling correction is not required but can be avoided if the spellings are irrelevant to the application.

We will discuss POS tagging, different parsing algorithms, and typical NLP applications in the next essay. We learned about the different pre-processing processes required and how the complexity of these steps varies depending on the language under consideration. As a result, knowing the underlying structure of the language is the first step in beginning any NLP project. Before we can teach the computer, we must first guarantee that we comprehend natural language.

What is Dependency Parsing?

The act of finding a sentence's dependency parse to comprehend the relationship between the "head" terms is known as dependency parsing. Dependency parsing aids in establishing a syntactic framework for any phrase to comprehend it better. These syntactic structures can be used to analyze a sentence's semantic and syntactic structure. The parsing tree may verify not just the syntax of the phrase but also its semantic format. The parse tree is the most often used syntactic structure. It may be created using parsing algorithms such as the Earley method, the Cocke-Kasami-Younger (CKY) algorithm, or the Chart parsing algorithm. Each of these methods has dynamic programming that can overcome ambiguity issues.

Because every one phrase might have several dependent parses, assigning the syntactic structure can get extremely complicated. Multiple parse trees are ambiguities that must be addressed for a phrase to have a clear syntactic structure. Syntactic disambiguation refers to the process of selecting the right parse from a set of various parses (each parse having a certain probability).

Natural Language Processing (NLP) is an emerging technology that derives various forms of artificial intelligence (AI) that we see today. Its use for creating a seamless and interactive interface between humans and machines will remain a top priority for today's and tomorrow's increasingly cognitive applications. In this section, we'll look at some of the most beneficial applications of NLP.

Machine Translation

One of the most significant uses of NLP is machine translation (MT), which converts one source language or text into another.

Types of Machine Translation Systems

Machine translation systems are classified into several categories. First, let us look at the many types.

Bilingual MT System: Bilingual MT systems generate translations between two distinct languages.

Multilingual MT System: A multilingual MT system generates translations between any two languages. They can be either unidirectional or bidirectional.

Machine Translation (MT) Approaches: Let us now look at some of the most important techniques to Machine Translation.

Direct MT Approach

It is the earliest and least common method of MT. This technique allows systems to translate SL (source language) straight to TL (target language). These systems are bi-lingual and unidirectional.

Interlingua Approach

Interlingua-based systems convert SL to an intermediate language called Interlingua (IL) and then IL to TL. The Interlingua method may be comprehended using the MT pyramid shown below.

Transfer Approach

This method consists of three steps.

- The first level involves converting source language (SL) documents to abstract SL-oriented representations.

- The second stage involves converting SL-oriented representations into the comparable target language (TL)-oriented representations.

- The final text is created in the third stage.

Empirical MT Approach

This is a new approach to MT. It essentially makes use of a vast amount of raw data in the form of parallel corpora. The text and its translations constitute the raw data. Machine translation approaches that are analogy-based, example-based, or memory-based employ an empirical MT approach.

Combating Spam: Unwanted emails are one of the most prevalent issues these days. This emphasizes the importance of spam filters, as they are the first line of defense against this problem. A spam filtering system may be created utilizing NLP technology by considering the primary false-positive and false-negative problems.

Modeling with N-grams: An N-Gram model is an N-character segment of a larger string. In this paradigm, N-grams of various lengths are utilized concurrently in processing and identifying spam emails. Word Stemming: Spammers, or spam email producers, frequently alter one or more characters of offensive words in their spam to avoid content-based spam filters. As a result, content-based filters are useless if they cannot comprehend the meaning of the words or phrases in the email. To address such difficulties in spam filtering, a rule-based word-stemming approach is being developed to identify words that look and sound identical.

Bayesian Classification: This is a commonly used spam filtering method. In a statistical method, the frequency of the terms in an email is compared to its usual occurrence in a database of unsolicited (spam) and genuine (ham) email communications.

Automatic Summarization

The most important item in our digital era is data, often known as information. But do we obtain valuable information as well as the needed amount of information? The answer is 'NO,' since information overload exists, and our access to knowledge and information far surpasses our capacity to comprehend it. Because the deluge of information on the Internet will not cease, we are in desperate need of automatic text summaries and information.

Text summarization is a technique for creating brief, accurate summaries of larger text materials. We will be able to find important information in less time, thanks to automatic text summarizing. Natural language processing (NLP) is critical in the development of automated text summarization.

Conclusion

Question-answering is another important use of natural language processing (NLP). Search engines bring the world's knowledge to our fingertips, yet they fall short when answering queries submitted by humans in their native language. Large tech corporations, such as Google, are also working in this area. Question-answering is a Computer Science topic that falls under the umbrella of AI and NLP. It focuses on developing systems that can automatically respond to queries submitted by humans in their natural language. A computer system that understands natural language has the capability of a program system to convert human-written words into an internal representation so that the system may create valid replies. Exact responses can be created by analyzing the questions' syntax and semantics. Lexical gap, ambiguity, and multilingualism are NLP's difficulties while developing an effective question answering system. Sentiment analysis is another significant use of natural language processing (NLP). Sentiment analysis, as the name implies, is used to identify the sentiments of many posts. It is also utilized to discern sentiment when the feelings are not conveyed. Companies utilize sentiment analysis, a natural language processing (NLP) technology, to determine their consumers' opinions and sentiments online. It will assist businesses in understanding what their consumers think about their products and services. With the aid of sentiment analysis, businesses may assess their entire reputation based on consumer posts. In this sense, we may argue that sentiment analysis goes beyond detecting basic polarity to comprehend the expressed viewpoint better.

<--END-->

www.ingramcontent.com/pod-product-compliance
Lightning Source LLC
Chambersburg PA
CBHW070845220526
45466CB00002B/891